The practical guide for the women who leads

Table of Contents

Introduction

The incorporation of women in new settings, such as the workplace and entrepreneurship, has focused on gender, female stereotypes, equity at work, and female leadership.

The definition of leadership that we present in this guide takes into account someone in a leadership position which is oriented to the development of people, the growth of themselves, the establishment of a vision that brings with it a greater good, to the search for a collective greater good through a benevolent, transparent, inclusive and positive guide.

Being a leader is a personal work. It is described as a process of building a specific role for mutual aid because a leader is not someone who is born with a set of particular talents, skills, and qualities. He is a highly results-oriented person who wants to create the best version of herself and share this with others through work, dedication, and effort.

That is why this book is not just any document; it is a guide that presents the characteristics, values, and competencies that an effective leader must possess. We take you away from traditionalist perceptions of what someone at the head of a work team does, and we give you the tools to transform yourself and the environment in which you operate.

We know that as a woman, you could be questioning yourself about your ability to take charge of your personal and professional life. Still, we faithfully believe in the power of the female gender, the benefits rooted in gender, and its strength to face the challenges imposed by a society in a complex and slow transition process. Thus, we hope you enjoy this book and can apply practically all the tips, advice, and steps throughout each chapter to act like the leader you already are.

PART ONE: GENDER AND LEADERSHIP

In a world dominated by patriarchy, many women have raised their voices and dared to lead groups searching for greater well-being. Getting to the true origin of who was the first woman to become a leader in the history of humanity is a challenge, but we can mention significant figures such as Emmelin Pahurst (1858-1928), a political activist who built the foundations for consolidating the female vote in England; Virginia Woolf (1882-1941), who dared to challenge social norms to sustain herself as a writer and Betty Friedan (1921-2006) advocate for women's rights in health, work, education, and social protection.

Lack of women in leadership positions

The current situation of leadership by women in the world leaves much to be desired. Although tirelessly, the female gender has managed to position itself more and more in managerial, power, or command positions. The truth is that they still exist many circumstances that can even be listed, which prevent women from reaching high positions in all areas of their lives.

Throughout history, an exhaustive number of social movements have sought to position women in areas that are not only related to the home, which became more evident in the last century. With their own efforts, women's fight for equal opportunities has improved the outlook for their imminent rise in the world's leadership positions, but this does not mean that there is already an assured victory.

It is clear that women's participation in workspaces and especially in leadership roles, has been increasing; however, the numbers are clear. Female gender participation is still minimal because, few females manage a company, reach executive positions or presidencies, even though they represent almost half of the workforce in the United States, this means that although a clear improvement in the positioning of women in professional spaces cannot be denied, women are still not adequately represented in leadership positions.

It is incredible to know that there are many prejudices related to women's presence in leadership roles even today. Some of the prejudices that women have to face are presented below.

Sexism

It is common to perceive women in leadership as incongruous people. Perhaps this is since people tend to imagine a leader in a generalized way with more masculine characteristics such as competitiveness. At the same time, women have a performance more inclined to the collective than individualism. These can detract from women's leadership capacity, as it is expected to see a dominant guide and not a caregiver. Later it will be detailed that both characters are not exclusive and that the nature of the female gender is, in fact, something very beneficial for the achievement of results.

Lack of credibility in leadership

This section talks explicitly about the image that women transmit. Although "dressing for the job you want" applies to both men and women, women are judged more severely for personal care and their sense of fashion. This diverts the attention of people who, rather than focusing on the results granted as a leader, evaluate women's performance based on more superficial topics. Simultaneously, for men, personal image is considered something of support for their performance and not something priority.

Communication as an image can also represent a disadvantage for women with short stature, delicate features, or high voices, which give an idea of being too soft and, therefore, not qualified to adopt leadership roles.

Doubts about performance

The exceptions to women who achieve a leadership position are usually low by stakeholders. It is generalized that women have their attention divided due to traditional roles imposed on female genders such as marriage, parenting, and the home, developing the belief that a woman will never give 100% of her capacity and performance in the position since women activities carried out in the leadership role are something complementary or not a priority within their personal development.

For this reason, most of the positions are designed for leaders thinking about the male gender, who actively participates also developing thinking related to their role of supplier affiliated with the male gender, which gives them the power to prioritize themselves in the ladder of the plan of career since their reason for existing in the position also coincides with their professional role.

The reality is that although every day, there is a constant fight against the prejudices of women, there are still deep-rooted barriers that do not allow the deconstruction of gender roles to achieve equity in the workplace.

The relevance of women in leadership

Why do we need more women in leadership positions? With the search for gender equality, it should not be essential to discuss women's leadership presence. The presence of men and women equally should be the most natural thing, but this does not happen in practice, and therefore, the discussion expressed here is essential.

The presence of feminist discourses should not only be part of a marketing strategy that is present in all mass media. It must be reflected in reality because there are specific reasons why women's inclusion in management is beneficial for all; these are presented below.

Leadership style

Women's leadership style is more oriented towards people, so mentoring and always coaching present in their way of doing things, unlike a man who tends to focus more on control. Again, equity and balance are being sought, and to obtain benefits from both, the balance must be adjusted through more inclusion of women.

Holistic thinking

Women have holistic thinking; that is, they perceive and globally analyze reality, which allows them to have a concentration that goes beyond short-term objectives and visualize them as part of a whole, as scalenes that lead to the achievement of a greater good. They can face future challenges because they prepare from the present to meet them, reducing the feeling of uncertainty. Women are something like accident insurance.

Engagement

Something that characterizes women is their empathy. This quality enables female leaders in leadership to trust all stakeholders: peers, subordinates, clients, partners, community, etc. The links that they generate with all the interested parties in the field they develop are usually long-term relationships because they can keep them engaged. They are an excellent public face for any institution or organization.

Equity

The fastest way to create diversity in workgroups is by including both genders so that the number of female contributors and female contributors is balanced. The representation of groups that today are a minority is a subject of great importance for all generations and represents an important point to increase the motivation of the members of a work team and accept the activities carried out by a group by members of society.

Sustainability

Some studies suggest that women have more developed interest in environmental care and management of resources for future generations. Because we are in a world that has been hit by negative impacts on the environment and threatens everyone's lifestyle, it is wise to put people who have an integral management style that allows generating the least impact on the environment when carrying out activities.

Innovation

The inclusion of a different gender perspective promotes a greater variety of ideas, proposals, opinions, and ways of interpreting the environment's variables. Therefore, the answers or solutions to current problems could present a breath of fresh air if the number of people capable of adding value from a different perspective increases.

Working environment

The last benefit that we show in this chapter is the evident improvement of the work environment, regardless of the background in which one works. Women with the ground that they have gained in the professional sphere have demonstrated, over time, a tendency to be more inclusive and more collaborative than the opposite gender. The trust and group harmony they develop in their teams make them actively participate and encourage them to contribute even when it is not an essential part of their activities.

PART TWO: ALL ABOUT LEADERS

What is and what is not leadership?

Leadership is a position, competence, and a process. In the first place, a leader is a person who is at the head of a team; therefore, this means that in a hierarchical scale, it is at a higher level; for example, in a vertical organization, it would be seen at the top and in a circular organization chart would be seen in the center of it. The leader is also the one at the top of the chain of command, and the main weight of decision-making will fall on this person.

Second, leadership is also a competition. Competence is defined as the talents, skills, and knowledge that a person possesses or needs to develop. Leadership is the ability of a person to be in front of a team and achieve that all members of this team share the vision established for a said organization, setting objectives that allow a measurement of the degree of progress that there is a certain period in the time to become what is proposed in the vision and also, to be sufficiently observant and inspiring to ensure that their subordinates can reach their maximum potential, in such a way that each one becomes a valuable element for the continuous improvement of your group and of course, the achievement of objectives.

Finally, leadership is also a process, since we all can become leaders through formal study, autonomous training, mentoring, experience, and very contrary to how you may have read elsewhere, the leader it is not born, it is made. How can you start a transformation process towards leadership? Congratulations! You are already part of this process since, by reading this book, you show your apparent interest in forging the best possible version of yourself as part of self-learning activities.

Leadership positions have commonly been identified as the ability not to lead teams but to exercise power over other people through a commanding presence, coerce, and even earn respect through fear. Although many people in command positions manage their relationships in the way mentioned above, these people are not leaders but are taking advantage of their nominal jobs to carry out activities related to their work that although on many occasions It can achieve results, this in the medium or long term can cause low morale, the inadequate performance by the members and the decrease of their interpersonal networks. Therefore, taking actions such as threats or taking solely punitive measures to control subordinates is not leadership but simply exercising authority.

What kind of leader would you like to be?

We have already described what leadership is, but does that mean that all leaders are equal? No. While it is true that there are clear definitions of what it means to be a leader, the reality is that in practice, the characteristics mentioned above manifest themselves with many variations. Here are some of the most popular classifications in the literature, which will help you identify which category you are in or the style you consider best suited for you and what you need to work on for your leadership path.

Autocratic leaders.

Those who fall within this classification consider that power is something that must be centralized; this means that when it comes to making an important decision, they take it directly. Similarly, the entire series of decision-making and the processes involved in achieving the objectives proposed within your work team are under this same person's strict supervision. Knowledge for autocratic leaders is an asset that should only belong to privileged positions, which is why the members of their team have little access to knowledge related to their work, limiting themselves to what is directly related to their activities. Although this type of person has its own category of leadership, it is very close to what a leader is not, or at least an exemplary leader, since it arises from very traditional work relationships and uses methods that do not usually have an outstanding acceptance among subordinates.

Democratic leaders.

It can be said that democratic leaders are people who divide power equitably among their work team members. It is expressed in this way because decision-making is a joint activity that allows everyone to express their opinions. Each proposal placed on the table to resolve problems or continuous improvement is taken into consideration. In addition, knowledge is also something shared. A democratic leader will make sure that his subordinates know her group's objectives correctly and have adequate means to carry out their activities. Regarding the results obtained, they usually offer words of encouragement or tools to work in the opportunity areas, which makes them something similar to what a coach would be.

Laissez-Faire leaders.

Freedom is the keyword for leaders who fall into this category. The members of work teams that have Laissz Faire leaders lack any supervision. People in command positions like this prefer to let their subordinates know what the proposed objectives and the expected results are, asking them to investigate on their own how to solve the activities and tasks assigned, as well as the necessary knowledge for them. Likewise, it is very common for others to be encouraged to carry out a self-evaluation rather than to infer their actions when it comes to both doubts and results.

Transactional leaders.

Transactional leaders manage to obtain the expected results through exchange relationships with the members of their work teams, this means decision-making and access to knowledge is directly linked to rewards granted to motivate their subordinates in compliance and performance, is that only after communicating the expected results, it also expresses the benefits that members that your group will gain by achieving them. Therefore, unlike the Laissez-Faire leadership style, a transactional leader will do extensive monitoring to ensure that what is delivered as an incentive is the right element to guide the work in the direction you want it to. As for feedback, it will only intervene directly when there are contingency situations or severe problems. Although it does not apply to punitive, negative results, it can make a reward adjustment by designing specific exchanges for each case.

Transformational leaders.

This style has been mentioned many times as the ideal type of leader. People with this style tend to completely change their environment to provide welcoming spaces full of understanding, support, and trust. A transformative leader cares about being a knowledge facilitator who has a more people-focused orientation than towards processes. Therefore, he seeks to support his work team through empowerment, inspiration, cooperation, and the creation of aspiration, establishing objectives, and achieving in all the group members to have a shared vision for achieving goals. Decision-making is consensual, and, if it is about results, they will very definitely not apply punitive means. Still, through their own example and the construction of strong ties between people, they will encourage their subordinates to work on their strengths so that everyone can work in a complementary way.

Do women have a leadership style?

In itself, it is complicated to observe in practice the mentioned leadership styles in a pure way, being able to observe in people in command positions usually a combination of two or more types. Another critical issue regarding leadership styles is that traditionally female and male characteristics can be observed. Given that historically the home's traditional roles have been granted to the female gender and supply to the male gender, it is common to find that society perceives certain behaviors as natural in one gender or another, such as being protective, understanding, participatory, and emotional for women, and strong, assertive, dominant, and competitive for men. Even though today we know that both sexes can have characteristics of both genders strictly speaking from the traditional perspective, this has helped the specialists of the subject explain more clearly, for example, the balance shown in a transformational leader.

In this sense, it is possible to perceive that women tend to have more common democratic and transformational leadership styles since many characteristics considered feminine are relevant to these styles. At the same time, each day, they are less afraid of raising their voices, being assertive, and provide firm and clear guidance such as in autocratic and transactional styles. Before, an autocratic one was seen as an ideal leadership style, which made the male gender have the perfect image to be placed in critical positions at the head of other people, in turn, made the few women who achieved position themselves as leaders in their respective professional fields, were under a lot of pressure and did not meet people's expectations, even if their results were equal to or better than those of men.

The answer to whether women and men manifest the leadership differently is very ambiguous. Many of the scholars in charge of investigating this type of classifications do not focus on gender but on particular traits to create styles. Besides, the challenge to the leaders, both genders assume that behave similarly as they pursue an ideal generalized by the community according to the styles that have already been mentioned. However, when it comes to subordinates' perception, it is common to find responses that lean towards the fact that women are more collaborative, cooperative, and democratic. At the same time, men have a more directive, competitive and autocratic style. Ideally, in the future, both genders will be aware of the importance of fairness, adopting a transformative leadership style that is concerned with embracing both poles within their people, acting in a balanced way, and becoming role models with followers rather than subordinates who communicate values and purposes with optimism and always worrying about individual needs as well.

Leadership values

It can be said that values are attitudes, principles, and behaviors that are directly related to the way we feel and act. The values that we share with our family, our friends, our co-workers, and the society in which we operate are directly related to the coexistence rules that allow us to live peacefully in a group. That is why we can hear that there are beliefs about what is right and what is wrong, about how things should be or what an ideal world would be like.

Leadership values are a significant influence when it comes to the values of an entire organization, as you've probably heard the term organizational culture. Organizational culture is made up of something more than values. Still, in general, they are the basis of it. These characterize how groups and individuals carry out their activities and responsibilities since they are the beliefs of what is right or what would be best for the organization. The stronger the values a leader possesses, the more influence he will have over subordinates, but be careful! Values are something that is not only taught formally. For these values to be truly useful, a leader must ensure that they permeate all his subordinates through example. Otherwise, the values embodied for your team will only be an ideal and not values in use.

According to the above, leaders are the guide that makes it easier for others to create a difference in their lives, translating into benefits for your organization, whether we are speaking professionally in companies and ventures, or on a personal level, like your home interest groups. Responsible leadership is always guided by commitment, understanding, and determination.

Examples of values

It is the job of a leader to select those important values to himself and his work teams. Similarly, it also falls within their responsibility to ensure that the members who join their team share these values or help them in the adoption and development of them. Although there is a massive list of values that a good leader might possess, a selection serves as introductory literature on this topic.

Respect.

It is the ability to be considerate of things and people that are different. Reaching a level that allows even recognizing their difference, acceptance, and interaction does not cause offense or damage. A leader must be able to respect others and respect himself, having a treatment full of empathy and compassion. In the same way, you must have the ability to earn others' respect through dignified actions.

Integrity.

Integrity refers to the constant determination to always do what is considered right. A person of integrity can face day-to-day challenges, remain strong in spirit, and faithful to his principles. A leader of integrity lives with rectitude, kindness, and honesty, always having a positive impact on others by considering their interests and feelings without compromising the productivity and efficiency of work teams.

Authenticity.

A person is authentic when there are consistency and congruence between what he says or preaches and his actions. She accepts her feelings and behaviors responsibly and is consistent with herself, and is also honest with others. To be an authentic leader, he must act with conviction and transparency, with fidelity to himself but always integrating the values with a purpose and contributing to others' growth.

Courage.

It refers to the strength someone possesses to act for the greater good. It is an exercise of will to overcome the barriers and obstacles that arise in achieving our goals and objectives. They always have their eyes fixed on the vision of what they want to achieve, which allows them to still stand up to the end. This leader stands firm in the face of adversity by acting courageously in the face of injustices and defending others.

Service.

Someone helpful will always guide their actions towards the benefit of others. People with this value are attentive, observant, and timely, so they know when the ideal time to help people out is. A leader guided by this value will always be committed to the cause before his personal interests, aligning them with the vision with the intention of going beyond individualism and acting with humility.

Humility.

Linked to the previous value, humility refers to modest people's characteristics, who do not consider that they have importance or higher value than other people, even when society defines them as successful people. A humble leader is aware of his own limitations and has an open mind to see situations from other people's perspective, accepting that everyone has the ability to evolve in life.

Wisdom.

The importance of wisdom lies in the fact that this value guides people always to give priority to knowledge, both valuing it and acquiring it, using said knowledge in a prudent and sensible way, always taking into account that they have been created for the improvement of people in your day to day. A wise leader knows in depth the dynamics of interpersonal relationships and how to balance people's interests to improve decision-making.

Cooperation.

Cooperation refers to the ability of individuals to work as a team, this seeking the good of all members of the team and under the scheme of other values such as respect and humility. A leader who encourages cooperation as a value recognizes the ideas, skills, strengths, and contributions of everyone in the team, through knowledge and socialization among its members achieved by implementing active participation.

Commitment.

A person who has commitment within his pillar of values is aware of the value of promises. Commitment implies speaking louder than words and prioritizing compliance with what is offered even if they are adverse or have limitations; that is why commitment goes very hand in hand with integrity. A committed leader recognizes the accepted conditions and the obligations attached to them. Therefore his decision making is always full of meaning.

Optimism.

Optimism is the source of human energy. The ability to visualize positive results for actions taken in the present is what gives people a purpose for their existence, and the ability to continue striving. An optimistic leader contributes directly to the growth of his team by developing its potential to achieve maximum performance. This is achieved not only through example but by finding the purpose of others.

The values mentioned are just some of those that a leader can integrate into his scheme of how to do things; we can also mention other examples such as calm, competitiveness, learning, truth, freedom, fun, security, determination, sympathy, justice, assertiveness, caring, hope, friendship, gratitude, patience, trustworthiness, enthusiasm, and loyalty. But the ten values mentioned in this book are the basis for the development of all the others, and with the time, you will notice that once these values have been developed, you will have begun to show evidence that new values are now part of your philosophy as a leader.

Becoming the best version that a leader can become is not only about reproducing the actions and behaviors of roles to follow, but about values that are part of its roots since, in this way, a leader can always act in a way that works for what matters most to you. A leader without values is like a map without directions. In short, when it comes to values, leadership should be something flexible that you do with people. The success of leaders lies in the implementation of the values through teaching, training, mentoring, action, and communication. In the third part of this book, we will offer you a guide to identifying your own values and aligning them with the leadership style you want to adopt.

Values: areas of impact

The descriptions of the values presented have an impact on different aspects: personality, relationships, and actions. Below is how the relationship between these values and these different aspects works.

Personality.

Here it is not only the personality of the leader but of the subordinates that matter. The purpose of the work team guides the scheme of values that guide the way of doing things of the people who make it up. This is manifested in a tangible way in the set of skills, knowledge, and experience that each person has, for which a good leader is curious to know in depth the people with whom he works. With this, they can understand what makes their collaborators work or what their passion is. In this way, they can identify an incentive to implement current values or identify their moral standards so that, if they are different, the identification of people with the team.

Relationships.

Leaders must raise their expectations and not be afraid to challenge their subordinates. They challenge the members of their teams to use their strengths to solve problems and master those strengths. This does not mean that it works so that some elements are better than others. It simply polishes the strengths for the common good, emphasizing the importance of not competing but collaborating, supporting each other, and promising future benefits at the individual level.

Actions.

The activities and tasks to achieve the objectives of the work team should not be perceived as meaningless, so it is the job of leaders to make their subordinates feel significant, emphasizing the importance of a shared vision. All people need and deserve to feel valued, both as part of a team and individually, and it is the presence of this feeling that will have a positive effect on the results obtained. This, through the exposed values that must be visible in the actions of individuals, if the leaders do not manifest these values, an environment of distrust will be generated. Therefore, a leadership style must always be based on a set of values.

Women and values

It has been found that women have a higher level of acceptance of values related to the achievement of goals in a benevolent way. Possibly driven by the struggle of women in their inclusion in leadership roles, many members of the female gender understand by the achievement of objectives the demonstration of their competencies according to the expectations of society. The benevolence, on the other hand, refers to the interest of women in the welfare of others. Leadership demands both perspectives to be effective, which is why once again, the importance of the female presence in the professional environment is demonstrated since the success of any work team depends specifically on the ambition of its leader to achieve something important.

The values that guide women during leadership are a factor in managing their own talents; specifically, women have a high attachment to excellence performance, setting themselves high standards, and even aiming for perfection. As a consequence, if a woman fails to achieve the best results for a role or job, she may drop out, taking the time to retake the opportunity until she carries out her activities in a way that is virtually error-free.

Skills for a successful leadership

Competencies are something different from values. It is the ability to make use of certain knowledge, skills, and talents to successfully perform specific functions in a role or position. Formally expressed, the competencies are the standards that specify the level of knowledge or mastery of the skills and talents that are required to develop the tasks and also that allows measuring the degree of performance that a person has when occupying said role or position.

The leadership position also requires the establishment of a group of competencies that allow candidates or occupants to secure or maintain their position. A woman in a leadership position needs, like any other leader, to know in depth the competencies related to her role to improve her performance and, specifically, the female gender can rely on this knowledge to be able to function better in an environment influenced by norms of origin. Patriarchal is based on biases and stereotypes. Here are competencies or skills that will support you in being a successful leader.

Communication

The ability to communicate is crucial for anyone who wants to become and remain a leader. Leadership effectiveness is defined by the ability to explain the ideas, expectations, vision, objectives, and necessary knowledge for your work team. That is why we will share tips that will help you communicate better on a personal level, verbally, and in writing.

Importance of interpersonal communication.

Interpersonal communication is one that allows you to build relationships; later, we will talk about the importance of teamwork, that is why specifically understanding the relationship between communicating, and people is an elementary pillar for a good performance as a leader. That said, the first thing to know is that communication travels in two different directions, one party emits the message, and the other party receives it through a channel, which can be verbal or written so that later there is feedback or reply to the original message. Being a great listener is vitally important, but it is the job of a leader to set the tone and pace of communication within a team. Every call, every meeting, every email, every message will be a reflection of the current status of the projects that are in progress.

Effective communication will allow you to avoid future problems such as misunderstandings, confusion, different expectations, and inability to socialize. Therefore, it is a basic tool to increase the chances of obtaining the expected results for each proposed objective and that as a team, they achieve that vision shared that is so desired. Before going into detail about the types of verbal and written communication and the skills required, it is essential that you know the following: you must know your audience, everything has a time, and a place, and how to communicate is important.

Know your audience.

What is the audience? An audience is a public that is destined to come into contact with a certain means of communication. These individuals will be the recipients who receive your message and, if there is effective communication, they will also interact with that message. An audience is not a generalized group of people, but rather a small population made up of people with certain characteristics in common. These variables can be age, gender, generation, educational degrees, work areas, roles, etc.

The importance of knowing your audience lies in the ability to design specific messages for them and also manage to select a communication channel that will work to deliver that message. In the professional field, for example, it is not the same to talk with certain departments, with partners, with salespeople, with clients, or with visitors. For example, you can talk about how your products are created with both a manufacturer and a child who is part of a school tour. However, the safest thing is that with the first you use technical language and also touch on topics such as costs, while for the child, a very general and simple description will be made about what is done in a playful and entertaining way.

Moments, channels, and places.

Not all news or knowledge sharing can be done anytime or anywhere. Specifically, when it comes to bad news, for example, this information can result in low morale, so it would be best in such a situation to think about how to mitigate the negative consequences before sharing the information instead of doing it immediately. In the same way, the safest thing is that the message is shared in a personal way, in a comfortable and private place, that invites the participants to enter the discussion and vent their concerns and concerns during the meeting and not with poor performance or sharing comments that affect the weather.

That is why the three keys are mentioned: when should I communicate? The opportune moment to do this depends specifically on the message that is expected to be transmitted; if it is necessary to take immediate action, it is most likely that it will be in the short term if, for example, changes are to be made, it is safest to do it gradually between long term. ¿ What means should I contact? Here it can be added that the audience is also important and that some feel more comfortable with one or another means of communication. Although the adaptation of people is of the utmost importance, the impact that one or another means of communication will have on them should not be underestimated, since, in the end, the effectiveness of communication is more important than imposition. Where should I communicate? There are spaces that generate security in people, and therefore, the leader's job is to know in depth his work team to identify where he should act when carrying out a communication activity. For example, if we are talking about work, it will be less opportune to appear at people's homes than at their respective offices or, if you are organizing an event, it will help to better visualize the ideas in the place where it will take place and not in the center of the job. Choosing the moment, the channel, and the place to communicate is something complex but that every leader can refine over time through their own training and experience.

Set the tone.

Have you noticed that some places are very serious, others are louder, and some are even relaxing? This is due to the tone or style of work. For example, when we are in a place where many punitive means are used, and the means of communication are too restricted, you are likely to perceive the tension in the environment and see few moments of talk and limited messages. On the contrary, you are more likely to hear many voices if a leader promotes active listening and encourages everyone to share their point of view.

The tone has a lot to do with how. A news day off, for example, can become something positive or negative according to the way you say it if while you say that there may be a day off but constantly mention the pending issues that are in process, it is likely that people do not receive the same mental rest as if you communicate it with joy. Likewise, the person designated for communication influences, it is possible that if you are the leader but always delegate the task of announcements to the second in command, the other members of your team do not see you as someone accessible and therefore, they do not come up to you often to talk.

Types of communication.

Interpersonal communication can be done in three ways, speaking, writing, or not doing either of the two.

Verbal communication.

Verbal communication or oral communication occurs in face-to-face encounters of two or more people and can be formal and non-formal. This type of communication provides advantages such as a quick exchange and immediate feedback. On the other hand, the disadvantages of this type of communication would be not obtaining results, especially when the meetings are not planned and therefore the loss of resources such as time, as everyone knows who has attended a meeting without reaching a meeting. Formal agreement.

Although speaking may seem simple and natural for everyone, not everyone has the possibility of achieving effective communication through oral expression. But this does not mean that if you are an introvert or of few words, you are destined to never be a leader, not to be able to lead a meeting or to hold a conference. The good news about everything we talk about in this book is that everything can be learned.

In order to improve verbal communication, it is important to be very clear that this goes beyond the exchange of words. It consists of the exchange of information to guide towards an action or the construction of knowledge. Mastering face-to-face communication also implies learning to distinguish when it is pertinent to carry it out and when it is not, as we mentioned in moments, channels, and places. The tone of your voice is important. Raising your voice is commonly a sign of sanction or serves to attract attention while using a calm or calm tone of voice indicates that everything is fine. Speed can also improve or worsen effectiveness. Talking too fast will make everyone feel uneasy and anxious; it will let you know that you want that encounter to end soon while talking too slowly can eventually cause them to stop paying attention. You must find the exact point that allows you to communicate things in a way that offers clarity in the message you want to convey.

Non-verbal communication.

Non-verbal communication commonly supports verbal communication. This is done through the body language of people, who, while speaking, make gestures, movements, and facial expressions that can reinforce their message, add information and even say something contradictory to what you are saying at the time. But this does not mean that non-verbal communication is secondary. In many cases, the non-verbal expression can be observed by itself and offer a lot of information. A person who is slouched shoulders and sitting in isolation denotes sadness, another who slammed a door when leaving a place communicates and anger and, one who is smiling while looking at his cell phone is most likely happy, and we even think that they are giving good news.

It is important to regulate non-verbal communication when, as a leader, you are communicating with someone else. First of all, act naturally; it will let the other person know that you are genuinely interested in what they are saying or that the encounter they are having is important. If you relax your body, other people will also feel comfortable and not pressured. Non-verbal communication says a lot about you as a person; try that what your body does while you speak is coherent with what you are saying; otherwise, you could confuse your recipients or convey that you are not an authentic person, you could not be saying the truth or humor that makes them uncomfortable.

In short, when expressing yourself verbally, you can support non-verbal communication by doing things like maintaining eye contact, showing a firm but not tense posture. If you are in an open or wide space, try to keep people's attention by looking at several people and not focusing on one, move around the place, point and nod that you agree or disapprove of what they are mentioning to you when it's your turn to listen.

Written communication.

Written communication in the professional field is formal communication par excellence. Examples of written communication are emails, letters, instant messages, presentations, checklists, job descriptions, speeches, and other documents. Written communication is one that is embodied through words and codes embodied in media that last over time, such as paper or digital files. In this sense, it has an important advantage over verbal communication, since the message is not ephemeral and does not deform as it passes from person to person. This makes this type of communication ideal for keeping records and capturing knowledge that you do not want to lose, such as procedures. However, these characteristics do not make it the perfect communication medium either, as it also has disadvantages such as contamination in the case of the classic use of paper or the inability to provide immediate feedback, taking instant messaging as an exception.

The points that must always be kept in mind for effective communication through written channels are: carefully choose the content, taking into account the purpose for which it is being created and ordering the information so that it can be easily consulted; select the words used in the message, again, remember that the audience must always be present in the mind of a leader who communicates and it is not necessary to choose elaborate words that are not handled in the daily vocabulary, since you want people to understand what do you mean; also be concise, do not lengthen the message more than is necessary; Finally, get organized, it will not only improve the quality of all the messages transmitted, but it will alleviate a great load of stress, keep copies, classify the information and save everything that can serve you in the future in an appropriate way.

Communication skills.

There are essential skills for effective communication when exercising leadership.

***Assertiveness.**

Assertiveness refers to a person's ability to communicate what they think, feel, want, or need. It manifests itself in the openness to express oneself, finding the perfect balance between passivity and aggressiveness. So every time the person delivers a message, they do so in an honest but respectful way.

One way to develop this skill is to think about conflict situations in any area of your life and ask yourself what your answer would be. The answers you articulate should require the appropriate use of non-verbal communication, repeating key points of what they said to you, paraphrasing, or asking more questions to confirm that you are interpreting what they said correctly and reflect on the feelings of both parties.

***Active listening.**

You will have noticed in the previous exercise that listening is the key. There is no effective communication without active listening by the leader. He must demonstrate that he has a high capacity for understanding since the purposes of listening are to collect information, filter what is important, develop ideas as well as being a pillar for respect.

To develop this skill, make sure every time you have to communicate with someone to maintain eye contact, make the other party understand that you are paying attention to them, and make a summary of what they are mentioning to verify the information received.

Probing.

Why is it important to explore? Because in this way, we can obtain relevant information from other people. Probing allows a leader to make clarifications of the opinions, thoughts, and feelings that other people have. With these new points of view, he can keep an open mind and think of different solutions for the problems or contingencies that his work team faces.

To be able to carry out a survey on a topic or problem, you should try to select your questions very well, so prior research and planning are important, it is also suggested not to use questions that can be answered with a simple yes or no, but rather It should also be sought to invite the people who participate in expanding as much as possible to collect as much data as possible.

Feedback giving.

Feedback is something that allows people to check that what they are communicating is being interpreted in the way they want by other people. In the case of the leader, he does not only need to get answers as in the survey, but he must also ensure that his subordinates receive an adequate response to what they also express in order to feel heard and taken into account.

To develop this skill, make sure you always give an answer in a short period of time, be assertive with your answers by constructively expressing your ideas and feelings, and always show yourself willing to collaborate and be part of the communication circle with the members of your work team.

Communication barriers.

As you can see, effective communication is a skill that requires a lot of individual and collaborative work. Although everyone is eager to improve in this area, there are situations that prevent achieving ideal communication. As a leader, you may encounter or even create situations such as lack of organization, inability to retain, lack of confidence, inadequately expressed messages, emotional blockage, cultural differences, inappropriate physical spaces, and resistance to change.

Do not let problems discourage you, better focus on finding the causes of them; if you look closely, you will find that problems related to communication can only be the signs that there are deeper problems and that require attention as a leader. This is very worthwhile because it is relevant to improve the way your work team works. Always remember that this is why the weak points or problems of a group, institution, or organization are called the area of opportunity. No situation is perfect, and this does not lead to analyzing the following leadership competency: adaptability.

Adaptability

If you are a person capable of surviving adversity through change, congratulations, you are a person with the competence of adaptability. Adaptability or ability to adapt means for a leader to have the ability to anticipate change, and this translates into functioning quickly and effectively in any context. For this, it is necessary to be able to correctly analyze the environment to reorient objectives and procedures when necessary.

Consultation and training.

For some people, adaptability comes naturally when they are involved in new or unfamiliar situations. Other people elsewhere need the training to develop this competence. In previous sections, mention was made about the importance of humility and wisdom. These values tell us in this specific case, that knowledge must be valued as an adaptation tool and also be willing to constantly learn, both from formal means and from other people; after all, we cannot know everything.

The search for help and training is part of any structure for personal development and, of course, leadership. The role of this is to make people competitive and valuable to a group. The benefits obtained from working in constant learning are satisfaction, motivation, the adoption of new ways of working, safety, and productivity.

Sources.

Training and help can come from different places. You can find valuable knowledge in:

- Your colleagues and subordinates: Humility reminds people that they do not know much more than they do. With this, it is also understood that pride should not be part of the characteristics of a leader and should recognize their own limitations. When you don't know something, turning directly to the people on your team can be the most immediate solution to an obstacle you are facing. The reality is that a well-balanced team is made to compensate for the areas of opportunity of others and to support the development of the people with whom it lives. Resorting to colleagues and subordinates can also generate a sense of satisfaction since they will feel that their mastery of some skill or topic is recognized, and their reason for being in the group is enriched.

- Experts in the area: Sometimes, the level of specificity of a situation that leaders face requires the use of people with a high level of specialization. These can be found in your own workplace, in entrepreneurship centers, or in other organizations. The advantage of turning to an expert is that you will gain in-depth knowledge of what you need to know, and many times their methods of explanation are clearer than other people's, as many other professionals and leaders turn to them constantly.

- Consultants and coaches: Sometimes, what is needed is some motivation and learning to improve the management of emotions. Consultants and personal coaches are an excellent choice for ongoing development because their training programs are generally tailored to meet the specific needs of their clients. This means that coaches first study your situation, your personality, abilities, interests, and objectives to achieve a redirection of your actions natural, fluid, and sustainable in the long term.

- Courses: It is normal to be inserted in the routine of our activities to stay a little behind on trends, the best, and new tools. The advantage of the current situation is that the courses do not necessarily have to be expensive, nor do you need to invest too many hours of your time in learning. Nowadays, with the digitization of teaching, you can improve your personal and professional training anytime, anywhere, or learn something totally new.

- Books: You have some free time, and you want to do something relaxing, but at the same time, you have that feeling that you should be productive—the solution: a book. Books allow you to acquire knowledge and talents at your own pace because you choose their content and the pace of reading. Written information is also an excellent resource to help you organize your ideas and highlight what is most relevant to you.

Time management.

For effective leadership, time management is another of the keys to success. There are many things that can be substituted or replaced, but what time? Impossible. Time is one of those variables that people cannot control since time cannot be stopped, not even encouraged or advanced. That is why an important part of adaptation competence is managing time correctly. Time management is a skill that can be used on a personal and professional level. There is no adequate method for it, so you must carry out trial and error activities, based on your personality type and your leadership style. What we can share with you are techniques to develop a time management strategy along with flexible planning.

Organize.

First things first, you have to make a list of all the things you need to do in the day. This list of things must contain the tasks that really need to be done. It must be something realistic and achievable, or even when you manage to accomplish a huge number of activities. Eventually, you will suffer burn out, and your performance will begin to decline. At this point, it is not yet important that you identify the importance of each of your tasks; just think superficially, everything that has to be resolved.

A great activity to get started is brainstorming. In this activity, what to do is to open your mind and think creatively. First, select a topic that will serve as a guide to start jotting down to-dos, for example, household chores. Second, you should focus more on quantity than quality; this way, you will have as many ideas as possible. Finally, write your ideas, no matter the medium. The important thing is that you can access this information so that you can continue working with what you have already done.

Prioritize.

Let's say that you already organized your day and wrote down what are the tasks and activities that you need or want to carry out. Now you have to identify that there are two types of tasks or pending: those important and those urgent. That is why once you have your list, you must reorder the activities in order of priority.

The urgent thing is that which has a delivery or expiration date, delivering it late will make the benefits of said activity no longer be seen or whose failure to carry it out will have negative consequences. The important thing is what must also be done because it is what gives the most benefits, for example, to a work team, but does not necessarily have a specific date to be done. Thus:

- If it is both important and urgent: it is an activity that should be in your first place of priorities, do it now!

- If it is important but not urgent: calmly plan your activities; in the next section, we will talk more about this topic.

- If it is something urgent but not important: The wisest thing you can do as a leader is to delegate these tasks.

- If not urgent and not important: These are activities that represent a waste of time, since they may not have to do with your responsibilities and should be discarded.

Planning.

Once you have your priorities well established, you can assign dates or times of completion for each of your activities. If you want to be even more efficient in this, you can, instead of planning one day at a time, visualize the times when you will do your activities for two days or more at a time. This does not mean that you must necessarily carry out each activity on the day it has been designated. Flexibility is an important element that allows you to have breaks and incorporate new activities that you had not previously contemplated.

Identify a medium with which you feel comfortable planning. Some people find writing by hand relaxing, and that is why they use printed agendas or even bullet journals, which are personalized agendas made entirely by hand. Advantages of this method are to be able to use the organization moment as therapy and to always have insight what is pending that must be completed but, on the negative side, you should always be aware of carrying the agenda with you to be able to review at any time that considers necessary the advance of the day. As for written media, we do not recommend using single sheets because you could have problems losing them, or they could not have an order or sufficiently logical. Other people prefer to use digital media, such as electronic diaries, apps, or desktop programs. Usually, people who are in the constant movement are benefited by this method, since even many of the programs have the ability to work in a synchronized way on several devices. But part of the disadvantages could be not having the list of tasks fully visible in one place, difficulties in using technology, or failures of the same nature.

Taking action.

It is time to take action. Let's review, it has already been defined which tasks are waiting to be carried out, they have been reorganized through priorities, and they have been assigned a date and time of completion; this means that now everything planned must be executed. Why is this part important? Because procrastinating is the least effective way to get things done.

Finding the concentration to do things is not easy; in this book, we suggest you use the Pomodoro technique to cross everything off the list. This technique is a time management tool developed by Francesco Cirillo in the late 1980s. It takes its name from the tomato-shaped kitchen timer (Pomodoro in Italian) that the creator of the technique used to develop it. It consists of dividing the time into fragments that last 25 minutes, and each of these periods is separated by breaks. Attention here because these breaks are not 25 minutes or hours and hours of scrolling on the phone. Each break is 5 minutes, while during the 25 minutes of work, you must act in a concentrated and intensive way. When you reach the four pomodoros, it is recommended to extend the rest to about 20 or 30 minutes.

Teamwork and team building.

If there are no people to guide, the existence of a leader loses meaning. A leader only exists thanks to his work team, and the individual and group results of his team members clearly reflect the effectiveness and style of his leadership. Well, they say that a good team impressively raises the possibility of success, and it is that, at the end of the day, people are social beings who need to complement each other to achieve goals, no matter how hard you work or how strong your determination is.

Building a strong team is the smart way to work, as it will allow you as a leader to better manage your time and keep you constantly learning. Where do I start to build a suitable team? The first thing is to identify those areas in which you need support. Defining these areas is easy if you first identify what you do best. Perhaps, for example, you are a very charismatic person who is good at sales, but on the other hand, accounting is not your thing, how will you keep track of your income? Answering questions like this each time you identify an area that is not your strong suit will be a great guide for making a list of the people you need to work with. Remember, complementarity is the key.

Remember that to attract the right talent to your side, and you must not only focus on what you are going to receive, you must also pay attention to what their interests are on an individual level, to ensure you have the ability to offer the appropriate rewards and remuneration. In the same way, here, the importance of values is retaken to ensure that the whole team can move in the same direction. The ideal is that from the beginning, your subordinates accept the values formally embodied for the team and your values as leader and person. In this way, you will achieve not only excellent synchronization but long-lasting relationships.

Positive relationships.

Collaborating strengthens work teams, which translates into spending time with your subordinates, not just listening but understanding them, connecting with them, and always keeping them hooked on progress. That others see you not only as a command post, but a key piece in the team's operation keeps them cohesive, which makes everything they do feel like something with purpose or meaning and keeps them energized. This also supports them to develop resilience in conflicts, since they know that they always have a place to use as a refuge, feeling strong.

Social intelligence is summarized in being empathetic and working productively with people with honor and respect for them and for oneself, respecting everything that makes them up, and being open to voluntarily listening to points of view before making any decision. This promotes positive working relationships that bring benefits like the ones listed below.

- The physical, emotional, and mental well-being of its members:

Every day there are and more studies that promote the mental health of people in the professional and personal sphere. When the identities created at work are positive, you get superior social and psychological functioning along with more positive feelings. Happy subordinates also improve their physical health since good emotions are directly related to an impact on the cardiovascular, hormonal, and immune systems.

- Decrease in conflicts:

Weak connections between people can cause conflict in teams or groups, as they generate feelings of exclusion, demotivation, frustration, or lack of respect. This not only causes a decline in the performance of the individual person, but it can also affect the performance of one or several groups. Therefore, positive relationships promote, through the recognition of interdependence, intention, and communication, restorative approaches that improve procedures and lead to the creation of constructive tasks.

Motivation

People are not motivated exclusively by extrinsic elements such as money. Lots of people are paid the right salary and may initially show incredible results, but if the deal stands alone in this way, it might not be very long-lasting, why then? People do their best only for intrinsic reasons, that is, those purposes and goals that people pursue. Therefore, if the vision assigned to a work team is satisfactory enough for a person, it is more likely that it will always keep developing at an adequate rate as opposed to offering only material goods.

- Innovation and creative improvement:

A leader always delivers excellent results, and these results are usually most easily seen through a competitive perspective. In a world governed by global competitiveness, the ability to innovate, and the ability to provide creative solutions create an advantage that manifests itself in added value. Creativity can be reflected in managing relationships differently. Similarly, the factors that contribute to innovative teamwork are job enrichment, a climate of trust, respect, support, active participation, and knowledge sharing.

Conflict management.

When you find yourself in the role of leader, the presence of conflicts is practically inevitable. Conflict refers to situations of confrontations and disagreements. They develop from living with other people in different areas where one of the parties has ideas, interests, or feelings towards something or a different situation. From that, a conflict is created as the shared vision is lost, and it begins to "walk" in different directions.

The existence of a conflict does not necessarily have to be something negative. It simply means that the time has come to redesign the way we do things and make changes in interpersonal relationships. Viewed this way, a conflict is not just a setback but an opportunity to improve. What should a leader know about conflict? That there are several of these and that the causes are diverse and must be handled flexibly and consciously.

Conflicts can fall into four different categories: intrapersonal conflicts, interpersonal conflicts, intragroup conflicts, and intergroup conflicts. Intrapersonal conflicts are those that occur within oneself. It can be something like not being able to decide between two different jobs or much more complex situations such as depression. Interpersonal conflicts refer to one that occurs between two or more people. The intragroup is what is developed within groups of any size, which can be from a work team to the family. Finally, intergroup conflicts arise between two or more groups that function adequately internally but are in disagreement with other groups, which can be political, religious, labor, ethnic, etc.

Identifying the root of a conflict is not easy, and the revised probing ability in the communication competency could be very supportive here. Some possible causes of conflicts could be lack of information, opposing values, personal problems, conflicts in the structure or organization, and different interests. Confronted problems must be resolved both individually and in groups, through a sequential decision-making process. Decision making is not always directly related to problems; sometimes, it has to do with decisions about taking new opportunities or adopting ideas for continuous improvement.

There are three models to resolve conflicts:

- Lose-lose: Unfortunately, in this model, none of the parties that make up the conflict is in a desired position. This causes that the conflict does not reach a real resolution and reappears periodically. This model is embodied in practice when both depart, renounce something that was important to them in order to calm the situation, try to lessen the differences by finding common ground, or simply pretend that the conflict does not exist and let the situation flow without intervening, hoping that time will fade the problem.

- Win-Lose: This is a more competitive model where only one party has a chance to get what they want. Normally this is obtained through tax actions such as the use of force, the application of more developed skills, or a direct order by a superior who dictates a favorable solution only for one person or a group.

- Win-win: This is the best result that can be obtained from working conflict, and it is acquired through collaboration and a true resolution of the problem. It requires both parties to acknowledge that something is wrong and to be willing to work through it by paying attention to the problem. The compilation of information in this model is key since the results obtained will determine action guidelines that allow the root problem to disappear.

Networking.

A network of relationships is a powerful tool that connects people from different groups and from diverse backgrounds. It is a process that consists of establishing and retaining connections with people who can contribute something of value to our vision, and, in exchange for that, one has to do the same for that person. The relationship between people and groups is given by projects and tasks in common, using all kinds of channels to maintain contact.

Personal networks give n to a leader the opportunity to share experiences, resources, and knowledge to collaborate and cooperate broiled to, through joint efforts, make a difference, meet objectives or contribute to a shared vision. Networks deserve attention because, through them, they are the ideal complement to a work team and allow the elimination of work barriers by being able to redouble efforts and knowledge.

The networking can be sorted by formality and communication channels. Regarding the first category, we can find that there are both formal and informal relational networks. The first classification includes networks promoted or led by formal institutions or organizations, which clearly and concisely express the communication mechanisms and objectives. The second classification refers to all those networks built by an individual throughout their personal and professional life. This does not have as marked guidelines as formal networking, but it maintains the basis of generating reciprocal relationships that add value.

The second category makes two classifications, networking, and physical networking virtual. The first category refers to the fact that there is a physical coexistence between the members of the network, so the messages can be reinforced with non-verbal communication. Trust is also fostered through more natural and close encounters because interactions allow for immediate feedback. The networking virtual does not promote such closeness between its members but instead allows communication anytime, anywhere, focusing on the message rather than the person developing the creativity of people.

There are four phases that allow a leader to develop a network of contacts:

1. Inventory contacts: When starting to build networks of contacts, the first thing is to identify who you know. Once this list has been made, you can proceed to classify them. This categorization of contacts is essential to identify which people or groups can add value and which cannot. An ideal classification would be to add descriptions and tags to your contacts that allow you to quickly access them as the situation requires.

2. Grow the network of contacts: This part requires a lot of trust, but it is worth it. It means being willing to make a speech that allows others to know who you are, where you want to go, and how you can generate value. Do not limit yourself to preparing only information about yourself. You must also carry out research work on the

contact you want to reach. In this way, you will show your interest in it and allow you to break the ice when making contact.

3. Find the experts: These are what most generate value to our projects; to get there requires permanent research work. To do this, one should not limit oneself to asking existing contacts. One must use other tools such as attending congresses, belonging to associations, making presentations, conferences or courses, and working on the power of the information and communication media.

4. Exploit contacts: You must both share and absorb the knowledge generated from contact networks. Any opportunity is good to learn more about your contacts and retain them, involving them in conversations and events in which you must also actively participate. Finally, remember, updating is the key to permanence, you must always remain flexible to modify or incorporate new ways of working, and as the objectives are achieved, these must also be updated.

PART THREE: DEVELOPING YOURSELF

The development of oneself is the most basic and most important thing on the path of leadership. If we begin to work on the foundations that lead us to understand leadership from the beginning, the process becomes an everyday thing and will eventually be part of our lives. Of course, we have to take into account that no default way tells us how to be an excellent leader; what we seek is to bring together the key features that lead us to our goal. Women beginning to take part in leadership more often in the society does not imply that men will lose their power in society; true leadership leads us to better options for all.

The development of oneself today revolves around educating, supporting, and developing future leaders in their lives, thus achieving the power to build their leadership according to their abilities. However, it is still common to hear the definition of leadership as the exchange of energy that exists between an authority and a subordinate, that is, a person telling another what to do for the simple fact of being above him. To erase this misconception is necessary to inculcate in the development of leadership, the courage and desire to learn, be curious, and understand the precepts that lead beliefs and behaviors in relationships.

Personal development

As life progresses, it is a guarantee to face a variety of circumstances, changing environments, and new roles that require adapting to them. A personal development plan will help you handle the pressures that come with continual changes and challenges so that you are well equipped to excel in all areas of your life.

Personal development is an ongoing process of self-improvement, whether in your career, education, personal life, or in all of these areas. It's about setting goals for yourself and putting plans in place to reach those goals.

There are many reasons to prioritize personal development in your life; here, you can find the most important ones that will surely convince you to start that change today.

Forces you to leave your confort zone

That physical and mental space in which you find yourself, the place that isolates the evils of the world. The comfort zone can become part of our daily routine, and although it is a peaceful and stress-free way to go through life, in the long run, it leaves us far from being prepared to face adversity, one of the most basic tasks of a leader.

If there are areas of your job that you don't like or are not good at, those are the weaknesses in which a personal development plan can help you improve. Tackling these areas and improving them can help you get out of your comfort zone. This will let you experience growth and improve your skills.

It's not easy to get out of the comfort zone, especially when we already have a mentality in which we are used to a life without obstacles, but thinking outside the comfort zone is what allows us to the experience of what we are made of and will help us to get ahead in the face of situations that may arise.

Develop your strenghts

A personal development plan doesn't only helps you improve your weaknesses; it can also help you develop your strengths. Taking the time to concentrate, to nurture and use more the things you are good at, changes something you are good at, and becomes excellent at it. You can reach a higher potential and achieve incredible growth in developing skills you already are good at.

It's an excellent routine exercise to work on your strengths every day. Remember that practice does it to the teacher, and in the world, it is not enough to have as much experience as possible to face the challenges both in your life and in an organization.

Increase your confidence

Making the decision to improve your skills brings you one step closer to feeling more confident. Once you have achieved one specific objective, acquired another skill, or developed a particular area of your life, you naturally will feel good with yourself. The more you continue developing the areas of your life that you don't trust, you will become more confident.

Confidence is believing in yourself, feeling comfortable in your true self, knowing that you are worth it. If you have confidence, people will believe you, and trust is attractive, brings success, helps connect well with others, and, in general, makes you feel happier. Only you can say if you have the confidence or not.

How to gain and maintain trust

Learn to like, respect, and love yourself - see yourself as your best possible version, find your strengths, feel comfortable with yourself, and love yourself for who you are.

Be social- don't shut yourself in, always try to have contact with people, get to know those around you, and try to find relationships that are worthwhile.

Do things that you are Good at - a quick way to gain confidence is to always do activities in which you excel. We are all good at something, and this is good for you, exploit it to your advantage.

You will feel terrific when completing a task that is given to you easily.

Pamper yourself.

Take your breaths, get some free time, a treat from time to time is good for the body and mind. Go further and learn to take it as things you deserve, your efforts should always be rewarded, and you do not need those rewards to come from others, but from yourself.

Accept that you and others are not perfect, anyone can make mistakes, but not everyone will accept responsibility - there is no such thing as a perfect person, but those who come close to being perfect are the ones who are able to accept their own mistakes and have the ability to admit when they are wrong. If you can understand that neither you nor the people around you are perfect people, you will be able to work more naturally. Making mistakes is human. Accepting and correcting it is also human.

Have gratitude.

Be grateful for what you have, of what you can do, of those around you. Gratitude leads us to humility and gives us a sense of joy in seeing all that we have to work with, both as individuals and for our organization. The opportunities that are presented to us are thanks to our efforts, but that doesn't mean we shouldn't be grateful for being where we are.

Improve your self-awareness

Personal development is intimately linked to self-awareness. It gives you the opportunity to honestly analyze the areas of your life that need improvement. Through this process, you come to know who you really are, what your true values are, and where you would like to go in life. Once you go through this process, you will improve your self-awareness and experience fulfillment.

You are the leader of your own life

The first thing we have to understand the training and development of our new leadership are our limits, starting with ourselves. We are the owners of our life, and therefore we must be responsible for it; we are the leaders of our own life.

This is a very important point to take into account, due to the current condition of society and how it has been developing in the past centuries, it's just beginning to be clear that things like gender, sex, social position, and status shouldn't influence a person's ability to be a leader. What if instead of seeing leadership as a relationship with others, we start by applying it in our own lives? The immediate result we could observe is what we do on a day-to-day basis will become easier to complete.

If we start with small things like setting goals for our day, our week, or for small projects and then keep going up until the structure of our life is determined by the goals we can achieve, we will eventually end up influencing those around us in a positive way. We have to always respect others but without showing fear of obstacles. We are going to give the opportunity to new ideas, to different ways of doing things, improving and being more efficient with us, doing things the right way, even if it is not easy. We can learn to abandon pessimistic attitudes, to care about others, and to surround ourselves with people who contribute to these goals.

It is necessary to get ideas out of our head that we may have preconceived of a society in which leaders are only seen if they are of a certain sex or economic situation. It has been shown in several studies that women are as good as men at organizational management, and in certain specific areas such as conflict management, they are even better. It's the right moment for women to start taking leadership positions to finally begin to see processes such as democracy and equality being used correctly, making even entire countries more efficient and fair.

Self-awareness

Current studies and the various ways in which leaders are trained today indicate that a leader must be self-aware in order to understand others. Key points of a good leader come directly from taking into account how you feel about the actions that are being taken. The most important points that develop from being self-aware are:

Empathy- Empathy is the ability to put ourselves in the place of other people to understand how they feel about a certain situation. The only way to develop empathy with others is by understanding how we feel about the things that happen around us.

Compassion- It is the feeling of pain or sadness that we experience when we see another person in a precarious situation. The most effective way to feel compassion is to have experienced a situation that puts us at a vulnerable point.

Persuasion- It is the ability we develop to be able to make a person think or act in a certain way through reasons or arguments that are not debatable. To persuade someone else, you need to communicate in a very personal way with others. Knowing ourselves and being able to express how we feel and what we want becomes invaluable when it comes to persuading.

Interpersonal relationships - relationships with other people must be based on feelings in order to communicate. It's simply impossible to think of being able to carry out a relationship if we are not able to express what we feel. Interpersonal relationships become a very important foundation for a leader. If we are not able to interact with other people, we won't be able to lead them.

These points make it very clear; our ability to know ourselves is completely dependent on how well we can connect with others. A true leader must be able to care for his followers; she must be able to help them to be better people so that they are consequently better for the organization of the group. Of course, getting into a new habit isn't as easy as being self-aware, especially if we've spent our entire lives ignoring the signs. Listening to what our being tells us about us on an emotional level is a very complex task that will most likely end up making a positive change for us.

Leaders who have developed their self-awareness in a correct and complete way have the moral obligation to care about others, which becomes humble people who relate to their followers, motivating them to improve, in the first instance themselves and as a consequence, to the organization.

Self-leadership

One of the best ways to develop innovative processes is through autonomy, that is, through self-learning and the development of our own leadership. The foundations of self-leadership can be described as charting your own path, following it, and even correcting if things don't go well.

Being a leader by yourself implies a lot of discipline and following certain concepts to develop the ability and to put it into practice in an organization. The most important thing is undoubtedly the ability we have to learn on our own. A good leader always has to be excited to improve, to learn what he doesn't know, and use it for the collective well-being. You must have the ability to set goals and achieve them, both in life and in your organization. It's very important for you to understand you aren't capable of doing everything and you have to be able to delegate and organize in a way to always be on the task that best suits you and your followers and more than anything, you must learn to always be focused on the goal and have a lot of discipline to carry out the tasks necessary to meet the objectives that are set.

Personal Brand

A good leader must have the ability to leave a mark wherever she goes; it's very important that she leaves changes in the people, organizations, and relationships she has since it's one of the ways in which the effectiveness of a good leader can be measured. One of the most concrete ways to achieve this objective is by developing a personal brand, a signature of your own, so to speak.

The personal brand is the combination of things that makes us original, interesting, and allows people to identify with us. The personal brand is then the perception or impression that can be had of us based on experience, competence, or the way of achieving our objectives within a community, relationship, or organization.

The personal brand is acquiring value as we progress in an organization or relationship. This it's the way in which superiors measure the impact that you can have as a leader with your followers. The development of your personal brand will be invaluable for how it influences the type of leader we seek to be, let's review some tips that will help you achieve your goal.

Acknowledge your passions

We can define passion as a strong inclination towards an activity that people like, and even love, which they engage in on a regular basis and two types of passion can be observed, the harmonious and the obsessive.

Harmonious passion occurs by internalizing activity within us and making it part of our identity, while obsessive passion becomes so strong that it begins to control us.

We had to make that clarification since the objective of accepting our passions must be focused on those that are good for us, and we must put aside those that could be consuming our life.

The ones you do with pleasure, desire, and pride; these passions can nurture and energize your actions. When we are doing something we are passionate about, everything becomes easier, nothing seems impossible, and most importantly, we do it with a smile on our face. If you need help to find your passions, think about past times when you have achieved your goals, think how easy it was, how satisfying the moment became when you made it, or think about times when you were so involved in reaching the goal that you didn't notice the flow of time. Those moments when we find our best being possible are referred to as being in the zone. If you are passionate about what you do, it becomes very simple, like something involuntary, this allows you to focus your efforts on being a leader.

Identify your values

Values are our standards and principles, our judgment of what is important in life. We must determine what our values are, what we consider good behavior to follow in practice. Values will dictate the correctness of what is wrong, and on many occasions, they will give us the guideline of how far we want to go if we find something that doesn't seem correct to us. It is very important to stress that drawing this line is not a sign of weakness; on the contrary, it is a way in which we decide from the start to where we are able to stop. Whenever this imaginary line is drawn well, and we continue to follow it at all costs, it's very likely that people will start to notice our character and personality.

Identifying our values is determining what is really important to you. A great way to start is by looking back at your life to find those moments when you felt really good, and you were sure about making good decisions. Find examples of both your career and your personal life when you were happy, proud, and you felt satisfied with your actions. What were you doing? Where you with other people? What other factors contributed to your happiness, pride, and satisfaction? You must identify the values you find in those actions in order to determine which ones to follow to achieve a permanent state of satisfaction in your daily actions. Curiosity, trust, generosity, grace, growth, hard work, leadership, compassion, balance, and ambition are some of the examples you probably came across while doing this exercise.

Once we have found the values that make us feel good, we must organize them in order of priority. You must do it very calmly and think about it very well since tomorrow you will have to make a decision and you are going to be required to stick to your values in that order of priority- Trying to make sure what you do is attached to as many values as possible. Once you have the list made, redo the exercise with the chosen values , and determine if you really feel good about yourself by following them in that order. If so, congratulations, now you just have to apply them in your life. You will notice very big changes in your personal satisfaction by sticking to your chosen values.

Set Goals

Goals are what take us forward in life; they are like oxygen for our dreams, the first step of every journey, and understanding the importance of having goals will give you a better meaning of life. An objective can be understood as completing a plan to obtain a personal or organizational result that we develop to achieve it. This means that any plan you make for the future, no matter what it is, is a goal. So even when you set out to catch up on your favorite series or do your chores, however small it may seem, you are setting goals.

Imagine being at a shooting range, but not having a place to shoot. What would be the point of shooting for no reason at random points? This is what happens when we do things without a goal in mind. It's pointless and a waste of time and effort. We can have all the potential in the world, but if we don't direct it to a particular point, our talents and abilities are useless. Setting goals for your activities gives your mind a point to shoot at.

Setting objectives also allows you to measure if what you are doing is on the right track since you have an endpoint and a comparison based on where you want to go. Imagine that you have to prepare five presentations for your meetings of the week, but at no point was made clear that they required the five presentations in any given time or order, you would be working without a clear idea of when to finish or what information you need to have ready for each of them. Having the information on the target lets you know where you are at all times, so you will be ready for all the work you may have to complete.

Goals also allow you to have better concentration and not be easily distracted from what you are doing. If you use them as motivation to achieve your goal, it becomes much easier to keep moving forward, knowing that you are close to completing it. In the same way, being concentrated allows you to ward off the ghost of procrastination. It's very easy to give in to distractions, especially if they become a pretext for not completing goals that you consider difficult. The reality is that regardless of the difficulty of the objective at the door, it will not be possible to complete if you don't dedicate yourself to it. Don't let distractions become an excuse for not reaching your goals. You are the leader of your life, and you have the power to decide when and how you want to do things.

Finally, the most important thing about having goals is that they give you enough motivation to keep going. Each goal completed, each advance along the way, generates in our body the feeling of achievement that leads us to want to continue moving forward. With this in mind, the positive attitude to see each advancement as an achievement is what you need to always improve.

So, knowing how the objectives work, it's clear we cannot get anywhere if we don't know where we are going. Goals must become a routine for you. What are we going to achieve today? How are we going to get to the point where we want to be? In order to always be able to move forward, it's important to convert our steps into the progress of objectives. It isn't necessary to set unattainable goals. Each step is a goal achieved. You have to set goals of all kinds, for example, that new language you have been thinking of learning for a long time, that book you said would read but have not even acquired. Skills are only learned if we develop them, and setting goals in everything is the most efficient way to achieve results.

Your experience is important

We can talk about two types of experience in this section, work experience, and life experience. Work experience will give you the practical keys to perform as a leader, and it's something we must look for at all times. The more work experience you can demonstrate, the more likely you will be given the position you require.

You shouldn't look for work experience only to put on your CV, but you should see it as the opportunity to be in a position where your ability is the right to be there and will be tested at all times. It's also one of the most important keys to being able to enter an organization. Studies show that more than half of employers are going to be inclined to hire people who have previous work experience, and this number will only increase as the positions become more important.

Work experience also can help you decide what type of work you want to do, and you can try for what you're made of. It's not bad if, at this point in the book, you are still thinking about what you want to do and where you want to go as a leader, so taking jobs that gives you practical experience can help you take the leap and find your place in the organizational world. On the other hand, it's the most efficient way to get closer to the other employees of your chosen environment. Remember, you are looking to be at the top of the industry one day, well first. You have to know what your colleagues think, and being there with them is the most effective way to earn them for tomorrow.

Experience can also help you finish finding those points you haven't yet fully mastered within the steps to being a good leader. Whether searching for a passion for pursuing or finding goals that will give you motivation, work experience will open the doors to see if the path you have taken is the right one for you. It's also the ideal way to test your talents and skills in the workplace. Finding a way to use them to your advantage is only going to happen through practice, trial, and error.

Having a job, regardless of the field, will also connect you in one of the most important networks for a leader, contacts. You never know when you will need someone you met at work or even how tomorrow those people can take you to new places and challenges. Contacts are something you must treasure since they become connections that are always useful for the development of your organization. You must also bear in mind that you can be useful to someone in the same way, and that is what makes it such an interesting social experience. Help others because one day, you will need it to help from them.

Finally, having work experience gives you something to write in your resume, something very important when entering an organization, so don't be afraid to start generating that experience and have the tools to help you get closer to your leadership goal.

Everything you've done so far has value. You have life experience and the answer to many problems; after all, the day to day gives us the tools to be able to solve adversities. Your experience becomes an invaluable asset for your organization, but it's up to you to learn how to use it for it to be useful. Although it doesn't mean that you should boast what you have achieved, it's very important you will be able to sell the idea that your achievements and experiences are the keys to reaching a new level for your followers. For your superiors, you and your followers are the keys to creating this concept. Your experience is worth gold.

Cultivate your skills and talents

It's time to take advantage of our skills and put them to use in a work environment. To be able to perform in the best way possible to achieve our objectives, we must always look for how to exploit the talents we have. If you are very compliant with your times, planning is perfect for you. If you like technology, dedicate yourself to ensuring that the tools are the correct ones for the development of the work. We are all different, and in a team, this is a good thing. It's very important to determine what your strengths and weaknesses are so you can make your workload revolve around it. In the same way, it's important to know how to identify this with the rest of your team as it will help to locate them where they best operate.

Let's talk a bit about the best skills women have to contribute while in leadership positions:

Thinking Ahead.

Starts with developing your short-term thinking and culminates with the ability to develop strategic and operational plans. This skill is very important to have the ability to develop realistic plans in terms of time and objectives with measurable results. A woman with the ability to think ahead must be able to devise plans, projects, and activities that will cover practical and creative aspects.

Get things done.

For this, we need to be able to locate the right person for the tasks and designate objectives according to their abilities. It can be said that the most efficient way to get things done is by putting the task at hand. People who are more in line with the task at hand will be much more efficient as they are always completing the tasks provided. An important part of all this is to be an active part of the tasks to meet the objectives, to lead by example.

Knowing how to take risks.

This doesn't mean that we should take risks left and right; rather, we should focus on analyzing risks and making sure that those taken are with a very low probability of failure. You must work with the mindset that luck is not always going to be in your favor.

Decision making.

The correct aptitude for this challenge depends on not hesitate too much when being in a dilemma and eventually being responsible for the consequences. It doesn't matter if they are successes or failures.

Have initiative.

Know how to be the first to start moving, without waiting for others. Having an open mind that allows you to do things that others don't think regularly or even things that haven't been done before, are the ways to be one step ahead of others.

Get creative.

Think outside the box. Your mind must be ready to take decisions and actions beyond the limits. You must believe that change is a good thing and necessary to achieve improvements. Being able to take the risk of doing different things and not being afraid to admit a mistake and correct it in case things do not go as expected.

Conceptualize.

you must develop the ability to draw conclusions from past and present experiences in order to apply what you have learned in future projects, try to always evolve and change for the better instead of using an approach in which things stay the same way if they are working.

Listen and ask.

you have to develop with your colleagues the idea that communication is very important, especially listening to the ideas of others, always asking for doubts or unclear concepts, and expect there is always feedback both in your doubts and in those that others have.

Teamwork.

We are not alone, and we must always work thinking that we have people around us with the ability to support us to achieve our goals because this is what they are, group goals. This skill also includes the ability to deal with possible problems that develop in the group—problem-solving with other members and with yourself.

Monitor and evaluate.

You must be able to allow the evaluation of the effectiveness and the implementation of corrections that allow the best functioning of the organization. Learning to develop tools to identify problems and take action on identified deficiencies will allow your work to flow and be efficient throughout your group.

Managing your emotions

Emotions can be considered as a subjective state of mind in which there are reactions to internal stimulation, such as thoughts or memories of events that occur around us. We must clarify that emotions are not the same as the state of mind, which is a mental state that predisposes us to act in a certain way. For example, someone in a bad mood is more likely to get upset if some money is lost, just as someone in a good mood may just take it in a funny way.

Emotions themselves are neither good nor bad. They are simply reactions; however, since they are internal, the way we react to them can seriously affect our actions and well-being.

Since emotions are subjective, many people discuss the way to categorize them. For practical purposes, we will divide them as follows and in opposite's ways to have a clear idea of their classification:

1. Joy vs. Sadness

2. Trust vs. Disgust

3. Fear vs. Anger

4. Surprise vs. Anticipation

Several authors consider these as the basic emotions, and the other emotions we come to feel are simply stronger or weaker versions of these eight main ones. For example, rage is a stronger version of anger.

Emotions and our bodies

Emotions are controlled by an area in the brain called the Limbic System. This System is in charge of releasing chemicals to demonstrate our different emotional states. So the type of emotion we feel depends entirely on the chemicals that are in our body being released.

Emotions being caused by chemical effects have the ability to alter our bodies. This is the reason why when we are afraid, we can feel our heart beating faster, while our pupils dilate and we even begin to sweat. It's also possible to use this information in reverse and in our favor. For example, breathing calmly and deeply releases chemicals that make our body relax, and the heart stops beating fast.

Emotions are very important to humans, and from the beginning of time, helped maintain the survival of the species. When we face danger, fear will cruise through our bodies, putting you on alert and preparing to fight or flee. Unfortunately, emotions can become counterproductive for certain people, such as anxiety, it can turn emotions such as fear into panic attacks making the body unable to react, or people with depression can reach a point where they are unable to feel joy, and since the chemicals that are generated by this emotion are very important for the body, it becomes essential to find a way to cure these conditions. The previous examples make it very clear that emotions play a very important role in our functioning, and learning to control them can be the most effective way to have an advantage over people and find our position at the head of an organization.

In today's world, a person in a public or power position needs to have the ability to keep their emotions at bay, or it can end very badly. The perfect example of this can be seen in the daily news in which we learn that some head of state, athlete, or artist in the heat of the moment made an inappropriate comment or reacted badly to a certain situation. This is an emotion not handled properly, and it will only lead you to have to apologize publicly. Of course, not everyone is so lucky, and jobs, contracts, trips, relationships have been lost due to lack of control.

The most important thing to understand in training to control our emotions is that we cannot just turn them off. Our emotions will always be there, whether we like it or not. So we are not going to sit around waiting for the emotion to just disappear. The idea that we can eliminate them is not only harmful, but it isn't maintainable. Emotions are part of the human condition, and the more we try to live attached to our beliefs and values, the more our emotions will present themselves to challenge us.

The step number one to be able to take control over our emotions is to understand, as we have already mentioned it, emotions are neither good nor bad; if we can experience all human emotions without labeling them as good or bad, we can feel a great weight freed from our shoulders.

You must not allow emotions to define you. At the end of the day, they are chemical states that your brain suffers and you, on the other hand, are a woman who has already formed values and tries to live attached to them, so emotions will come and go. If you can successfully identify your emotions for what they are, you will have overcome the barrier of seeing yourself identified as a person dominated by their emotions. You will no longer be the one who is easily upset, the one who is always happy, or the one that everyone sees sad, scared, and confident.

To say we overcome the phase of the control of emotions, we must be able to think as follows. If an emotion is too strong and dominates us, we must find how to tell our body that there is an alternative. If we are afraid of speaking in public, it is something understandable, it is not a skill with which one is born or has experience followed, but if we can analyze it and decide how to face that fear, how to find a way to take a step forward, you will be controlling your body and your emotions on the path required to be a great leader.

Emotional Resilience

Up in the face of adversity. A persistent woman is focused on the goal and trusts the path to achieve it. Resilient people don't feel that things are unattainable or that the effort is pointless; it's very likely that they simply keep moving towards the goal even when they run into obstacles.

Resilient people are used to seeing things optimistically; this is a great advantage over others since seeing problems optimistically takes them above those who see situations as if they were victims of the calamity.

Resilient people have learned that support with trusted people is very useful to cope with problems; this point is very interesting since resilient people are characterized by being individually strong people, but it doesn't imply they cannot rely on close people in adverse situations, giving them better chances of success in the face of obstacles when achieving their goals,

The sense of humor plays a very important role for resilient people; it's always good to have the ability to laugh at adversity;

after all its, not the same to see things as a threat to see them as a challenge; this makes the body react differently to stress and let's not forget that a good laugh has many benefits for us.

Resilient people are able to see things in perspective; this means that they can, at the very least, learn from mistakes, see obstacles as challenges, and not allow adversity to get the best of them. People with perspective are able to see adversity as personal challenges and obstacles, while people who are easily stressed see it as the victims of their own bad luck.

Improving our resilience must become a daily exercise in which we seek to face each moment of stress in the calmest and efficient way. So you can improve this skill, you can work on the following points:

Connect with other people - give priority to your relationships and seek to join diverse groups that allow you to be in contact with more people.

Manage your thoughts - always seek to operate in one positive thought and get used to the idea that changes and obstacles are a regular part of life.

Take care of yourself - the most important thing about seeking greater resilience is to be well both physically and mentally. So you want to eat healthily and avoid exposing yourself to negative situations.

PART FOUR: MINDSETS FOR LEADERS

The lack of representation of women in various spaces is since our society has been founded on people's biological differences. Thought schemes were created that belong to the group of women or men, causing one or the other to have specific ideas, characteristics, and behaviors; this directly affects how they develop within groups, spaces, and different dimensions, emerging both female and male stereotypes. Social imaginaries are created through socialization and from there, an awareness of oneself and the other. In a generalized way, the woman is guided by a path focused on roles that have to do with couple relationships, motherhood, and the home in general. At the same time, the man is encouraged to adopt a supplier role. Although this seems to be taken from a film from the 1950s, the truth is that families continue to transmit this type of competition during their upbringing and other institutions also continue to reproduce these dynamics.

Delete the barriers of women leadership

Specifically, in terms of leadership, as mentioned previously, men and women find themselves in different positions within society, because although new opportunities have indeed opened up for the female gender, these doors and windows are still not enough to balance the balance of representation of both genders in the professional field. That said, it is important to highlight two things, thought patterns matter, and socialization and role models are the primary influence when it comes to empowering women to take leadership positions.

Thought patterns are directly linked to both female and male stereotypes and are the first thing you must change to become a leader. These thinking schemes vary according to the culture of your environment, but some globally recognized are:

I have to choose between family and work

The idea.

One of the main barriers to date between women and leadership is the impact that family responsibilities have in the professional sphere. Women are the central pillar of the family. Therefore, their presence and participation in household responsibilities are vital and not interchangeable; this means that people have lower expectations regarding women's professional performance, limiting not only their promotion to leadership positions but even their incorporation into the workforce.

Reality.

Women are no less efficient in the labor field because they have family and household responsibilities. They simply organize their personal and professional tasks and to-dos in a different way. In addition, although it is not yet a generalized situation, man is becoming more present in the home scene every day, gradually but consistently achieving balance the weight of home responsibilities, which will not only allow reducing the number of sacrifices that Women many times do to achieve their perfect balance but eliminate the stereotype since both, both men and women, will have similar backgrounds.

The woman is made to be subordinate

The idea.

This scheme of thought has its origin in the aforementioned traditional roles in which the female gender is dedicated to her home and the male gender as the provider, creating a self-perception of the woman of inferiority with respect to her capacity for economic activity, seeing themselves as part of a secondary or support workforce group.

Reality.

A woman has the same capacity as a man to perform in a leadership position. The gift of command, charisma, organizational skills, and other typical characteristics of a leader that we will mention later is not linked to gender, but to the mentality and the correct attitude to face the challenges that the professional world presents.

Being a leader is not feminine

The idea.

In general, women are educated to have specific characteristics and behaviors, and it is very common to find that they are educated under the notion that they should be docile, loving, calm, peaceful, etc. It is common to find situations where the leader cannot strictly adhere to these characteristics and must show a more aggressive, authoritarian, and imposing side, which is more associated with masculine behaviors.

Reality.

Don't try to be a man. The main mistake women make when they reach leadership positions is trying to meet people's expectations by adopting traditionally masculine attitudes. In this book, you will see that authenticity is the key to inspiring others and guiding them towards a shared mission.

I have to be able to do it all

The idea.

Again, society's low expectations about the role of the female gender in women make many women willing to move heaven, sea, and earth and even a little more to perform 100% with all and absolutely all aspects of their lives. Women have been presented, as part of female empowerment, that they have the ability to have absolutely everything: jobs, business, partner, children, beauty, health... and all this in perfect balance.

Reality.

Stop obsessing over the idea of being the best in all aspects of your life. Neither women nor men have the ability to have everything that most people dream of. It is true that the best thing you can do with your life is to always put your heart into things and give your best effort. But if you don't prioritize, the only goal you'll meet is to reach the burnout point. Define what aspects of your life are really important and dedicate yourself to more specific things. Focus on goals, not appearances.

The other important point that we touch when talking about women's representation in the professional sphere is the importance of socialization and role models. The exposure of women to leadership has a great positive impact on their perception of their abilities to become leaders. The earlier this exposure, the better, but this does not mean that if in your childhood you were not told all the time how intelligent you are and your ability to lead, you can no longer do it today. Interpersonal relationships serve as an important scaffolding in every woman's life, and connecting with the right people is critical when it comes to career advancement. For example, Jim Rohn refers to the fact that you are the average of the five people with whom you spend the most time since the mentality is contagious. The best thing you can do in cases like this is to surround yourself with high-performance women and high expectations. This will help you reach your full potential and perform effectively in leadership positions; this is where the importance of role models comes in.

The presence of strong women shapes the way other women who live with them view leadership: the key is trust. Living with other women who have assumed and made the leadership role their increases the confidence that any woman can be part of that group, especially when the women to follow are also good leaders and recognize the other women who do an excellent job, appreciate them, celebrate them and reward them. Does this mean that I should wait for a woman to present me with an opportunity? No, be the owner of your career:

- Dare to ask for sponsorships.

- Find mentors who strengthen their skills and talents.

- Ask for access to leadership positions.

- Look for job opportunities that go beyond your experience.

- Request a career plan.

- Mention that you want a promotion or a new position.

- Take the risk to undertake.

To start charting your path to leadership, you must replace your mentality with one that is not limited by expectations and stereotypes, surround yourself with successful people (especially women) with the ambition to improve and grow, plan your journey step by step, and create a suitable network to learn more.

I define mindset as the attitudes, beliefs, and expectations that you have that act as the foundation for who you are, how you lead, and how you interact with your team.

Your way of thinking is so influential because it determines how you think and interprets situations, your emotional reactions, the decisions you make, and your actions. Your mindset directly impacts the quality of your relationships, the interactions you have, and the way you lead. It also sets the tone for your organization and determines your people's kinds of experiences in their work lives.

Your mindset isn't just a bunch of sensible psychology and relationship stuff. It also has a huge effect on your business's bottom line, setting the stage for your performance, productivity, and, ultimately, your profitability. Your goal is to identify and create a productive mindset that results in privileged leadership.

The right mentality

Obtaining the right mentality will depend a lot on the way you want to approach your new life as a leader; these are some of the important points to take into account to have a correct mentality while in a leadership position.

Vision and performance

In the fast-paced business world we live in now, it's easy to get caught up in the daily challenges of running a business. The problem is if you keep busy in the machinations of the everyday corporate life, you may forget to look forward and to see what will happen if you stay on the actual course. What lies ahead can be a great opportunity waiting to be seized or a collision of several cars that should be avoided. In any case, if you are not looking at the horizon, the future will become the present without you being prepared to it.

That is where the vision comes to your agenda. A great leader cannot just be paying attention to the present. I focus on achieving my immediate goals to the best of my ability. A myopic view of your corporate world will only result in slow and painful corporate death.

Because true success in the corporate world is not judged by year or even by decade, your vision of the future of your business and your industry is paramount. Our success depends on always looking for what's next for our company. Recognizing trends, creating new products and services, identifying new markets, and predicting future threats are just a few of the ways that a clear vision can help ensure your company's long-term viability.

It's a no-brainer that great leaders should not only "speak as they speak," but also "stay on course" when it comes to their job responsibilities. If you want your team to perform at the highest level, you must first be at your highest level. The reality is that good is no longer good enough in the global and connected business world. Economic instability and competition from around the world means what was once enough to succeed now only guarantees failure.

The most successful leaders and companies know that nothing but the best is good enough to survive in today's business world. As a leader, you must speak up and show that you are constantly looking to take performance to the next level.

Responsibility and commitment

This mindset implies the degree of responsibility you are willing to assume in your company's role. Most company members primarily play the role of collaborator where they might say: I know my role, and I do what I have to do to fulfill those responsibilities. This mentality is clearly not the right one and won't allow them to obtain the leadership.

You should assume the role of the owner who says: Never assume that others are responsible. I am responsible for everything. Failure of others is a failure of mine. As an owner, you take the lead in all aspects of the company's operation and performance (or its team within the company).

The foundation of leadership is a determined and unwavering commitment to lead, perform, and succeed. The amount of commitment you bring to your role sends a powerful message of commitment to those you work with. Being motivated is not enough that will only lead to the fundamentals of business success. As a leader, you must be passionate, which means that you are really driven to excell. You have to prove your compromise to do everything the best way possible and go beyond expectations.

Principal mindsets

Gottfredson and Reina, a pair of Harvard researchers, found a pretty interesting way to describe what kind of mindset you want to develop to help your organization in a certain required way. You can focus on applying it depending on the way you require the organization to move for the overall benefit.

Mindsets are leaders' mental lenses that dictate what information they take and make sense of and navigate their situations. Simply put, mindset drives what leaders do and why. For example, they explain why two different leaders may encounter the same situation (for example, a conflict of interest) and process and respond to it very differently. A leader might see the situation as a threat that hinders his authority and another opportunity to learn and develop further. When leadership development efforts ignore mindsets, they ignore how leaders view and interpret problems and opportunities like this.

Growth and fixed mindset.

A growth mindset is a belief that people, including yourself, can change their talents, skills, and intelligence. In contrast, those with a fixed mindset dont believe that people can change their talents, abilities, and intelligence. Decades of research have found that those with a growth mindset are more mentally prepared to address and take on challenges, harness feedback, adopt the most effective problem-solving strategies, provide developmental feedback to subordinates, and be hard-working and persistent in the pursuit of achieving goals.

Deliberative and Implementation Mindsets.

Leaders with this mindset are highly receptive to all the information around them and often use it to the best use of it. On the other hand, leaders who have an implementation mindset focus much more on decision making, closing them off to new information that may allow for different ideas. Of the two ways of thinking, people who go for the deliberative part tend to make better decisions thanks to their impartial point of view and are open to observing all the information and processing it to make the appropriate decision.

Learning and Performance Mindsets.

A learning mindset involves being motivated to increase proficiency and master something new. A performance mindset involves being motivated to obtain favorable judgments (or avoid negative judgments) about one's competence. Compared to those with a performance mindset, leaders with a learning mindset are more mentally prepared to increase their competence, engage in deep-level learning strategies, seek feedback, and try harder. They are also persistent, adaptable, willing to cooperate, and tend to perform at a higher level.

Promotion and Prevention Mindsets.

Leaders with a promotion mindset focus on winning and winning. They identify a specific purpose, goal, or destination and prioritize progress toward that goal. Leaders with a preventive mindset, however, focus on avoiding losses and preventing problems at all costs. Research has found that those with a promotion mindset are more prone to positive thinking, more open to change, more likely to persist despite challenges and setbacks, and demonstrate higher levels of task performance and innovative behaviors compared to leaders with a prevention mindset.

Once you have a better understanding of these mindsets, you can adapt the needs of leadership to unlock your organization's hidden potential. A great example of an organization that harnessed the power of mindset in this way is Microsoft. Between 2001 and 2014, Microsoft's market capitalization and share price remained largely the same. But in 2014, when Satya Nadella took over, his mission was to renew Microsoft's leadership and culture. In his book, Hit Refresh, Nadella explains that the mindset, particularly the growth mindset, was his primary focus when revamping Microsoft. With this leadership, the company's market capitalization and share price have more than tripled.

This is just one example that shows that if s leaders of how to want their work effort go further, it is essential to give priority to the development of the mind, specifically the focus on attitudes growth, learning, discussion, and promotion. As leaders cultivate each of these, their thinking, learning, and behavior will naturally improve because they see and interpret their situations more effectively.

Final comments

We know that you could have finished reading this book still with many questions, so in each written paragraph, we have motivated you to continue reading to continue training on your way to being the best leader you could imagine. This is just the beginning of your journey to personal and professional success, and each word written here is one more building block for your personal development. Just as you probably still have questions, we know for sure that right now, you must be certain that in the future, the gap that exists between you and the role of a leader has decreased significantly.

We start the tour with a brief look at the importance of the female gender in leadership roles and what is your current situation in contrast to that. Then we stopped to do an exhaustive review that allows us to identify the true leaders and learn from the best practices, identifying useful values, competencies, and tools. The tour closes with the way in which all this knowledge enters your life to transform it, allowing you to be aware of your strengths and areas of opportunity and establishing a clear vision that you want it for yourself as a leader and how to achieve it.

Society is still in a transition period where the importance of the female presence in leadership is not yet understood. That is why it is your job, responsibility, and right to spread the word and share this information with other women who you think need a push or motivation to become agents of change. The challenge for women is to recognize their difference as a source of strength and courage. They must embrace their gender as something positive that makes their leadership practices unique. You will see how, in the short term future, this will be a competitive advantage. We close this book hoping that you have taken the knowledge that has permeated enough to accompany you throughout your life and with enough motivation to turn everything into concrete actions.

REFERENCES

Afkhami, M., Eissenberg, A., & Baziri, H. (2001). *Leading to Choices: A Leadership Training Handbook for Women.* Maryland, USA: Women's Learning Partnership for Rights, Development and Peace (WLP).

Barcelona Activa. (2010). *Cápsula de conocimiento: Networking.* Adjuntament de Barcelona. Retrieved from: https://treball.barcelonactiva.cat/porta22/images/es/18_Network ing_ES_Intranet_P22_tcm24-3811.pdf

Contreras, F., Pedraza, J. & Mejía, X. (2012). Women and Business Leadership. *Divérsitas: Perspectivas en Psicología. 8* (1), 183-194.

Corneau, G. (2004). *Networking: La gestión del conocimiento de las redes organizacionales.* Fundació per a la motivació dels recursos humans. Retrieved from: https://factorhuma.org/attachments_secure/article/8318/Network ing_cast.pdf

Gottfredson, R. & Reina, C. (2020). To Be a Great Leader, You Need the Right Mindset. USA: Harvard Business Review. Retrieved from: https://hbr.org/2020/01/to-be-a-great-leader-you-need-the-right-mindset

Internation Labour Office. (2005). Leadership Training Manual for Women Leaders of Cooperatives. India. Retrieved from: https://www.ilo.org/wcmsp5/groups/public/---asia/---ro-bangkok/---sro-new_delhi/documents/publication/wcms_124337.pdf

Lau, J. (2011). *Woman and Leadership: Transforming Visions and Current contexts*. Forum of Public Policy. Retrieved from: https://files.eric.ed.gov/fulltext/EJ944204.pdf

Moncayo, B. & Zuluaga, D. (2015). Leadership and Gender: Female Barriers in Academic Administration. *Pensamiento & Gestión. 39*, 142-177.

Rehman, A. (2014). Role of Training and development in an Organization. SSRN. Retrieved from: https://ssrn.com/abstract=2480345

Roffey, S. (2016). *Positive Relationships at work*. In Book: The Wiley Blackwell Handbook of the Psychology of Positivity and Strengths-Based Approaches at Work (pp.171-190). USA: Wiley.

Tarr-Whelan, L. (2009). *Women Lead the Way: Your Guide to Stepping Up to Leadership and Changing the World.* [EPub], Berret-Koehler Publishers.

Tarruella, R. (2019). Leadership Strategies: Learn the critical 5-steps to becoming an effective leader that your market will follow! Independently Published.

Veihmeyer, J. & Doughtie, L. (2015). *KPMG Women's Leadership Study: Moving Forward into Leadership Roles.* USA: KPMG International Cooperative.

Wittenberg, L. (2016). *Become the Leader you are: Self-Leadership Through Executive Coaching* (2nd Edition). [EPub], Bookboon.com.

Women's Coalition of of Zimbabwe. (2019). *Strengthening Women's Leadership in Training Manual.* [EPub], Hivos: People Unlimited.

Zydziunaite, V. (2018). Leadership Values and Values Based Leadership: What is the Main Focus? *Applied Research in Health and Social Sciences: Interface and Interaction. 15* (1), 43-58.